Hi! My name is Sophi. I'm here to say hello. And talk to you about my autism.

I may behave differently than some children. And that's because of some unique needs.

And it is all right!
Like everyone else, I
am a kind person
who wants to share
my love with others.

Time for recess Sophi!

I don't always comprehend things well, so please be patient.

Sometimes, we all need assistance. I'll eventually understand!

I sometimes take my shoes off and stand on my toes as I walk. My toes like the feeling.

Sometimes, I think I can reach the sky.

At times I like to play by myself. It helps me think and calm down.

I love my Play-Doh

I can make anything out of it, and it's squishy.

My task board is fantastic!
The gadgets rotate, light up, and make noises.

I often repeat words.

Let's go Let's go

But the reason for it is that I want to show you something.

People might be unsure of how they can communicate with me but don't worry.
Just ask my parents or teacher, and they'll explain!

Thank you for believing in me and for showing me care.
I we can play and be friends. Lets enjoy ourselves together.